Date: 5/10/17

Hh

Bela Davis

Abdo
THE ALPHABET
Kids

abdopublishing.com

Published by Abdo Kids, a division of ABDO, PO Box 398166, Minneapolis, Minnesota 55439.
Copyright © 2017 by Abdo Consulting Group, Inc. International copyrights reserved in all countries.
No part of this book may be reproduced in any form without written permission from the publisher.

Printed in the United States of America, North Mankato, Minnesota.

102016

012017

THIS BOOK CONTAINS
RECYCLED MATERIALS

Photo Credits: iStock, Shutterstock

Production Contributors: Teddy Borth, Jennie Forsberg, Grace Hansen

Design Contributors: Christina Doffing, Candice Keimig, Dorothy Toth

Publisher's Cataloging in Publication Data

Names: Davis, Bela, author.

Title: Hh / by Bela Davis.

Description: Minneapolis, Minnesota : Abdo Kids, 2017 | Series: The alphabet |
     Includes bibliographical references and index.

Identifiers: LCCN 2016943888 | ISBN 9781680808841 (lib. bdg.) |
     ISBN 9781680795943 (ebook) | ISBN 9781680796612 (Read-to-me ebook)

Subjects: LCSH: English language--Alphabet--Juvenile literature. | Alphabet
     books--Juvenile literature.

Classification: DDC 421/.1--dc23

LC record available at http://lccn.loc.gov/2016943888

Table of Contents

Hh

Hugo and **H**elen **h**ave fun.

Hh

Henry **h**angs in a **hammock**.

Hh

Harry **h**ides from **h**is friend.

Hh

Harper **hikes** wit**h h**er family.

Hh

Hal and **H**anna **h**old **h**ands.

Hh

Holly **h**as a **h**ula **h**oop.

14

Hh

Hope **h**elps **h**er mom.

Hh

Hector **h**ugs **h**is dad.

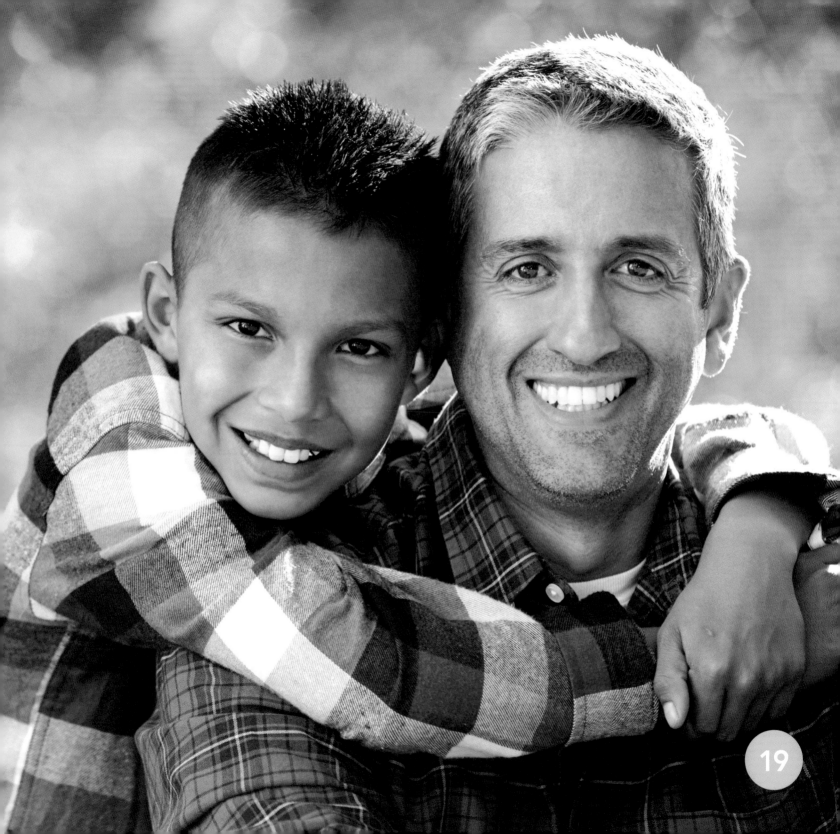

Hh

What does **H**ailey ride?

(a **h**orse)

More Hh Words

hamburger

helicopter

heart

hippo

Glossary

hammock
a hanging bed attached to supports at each end.

hike
to walk a long distance, especially for pleasure.

Index

abdokids.com

Use this code to log on to abdokids.com and access crafts, games, videos, and more!

Abdo Kids Code:
THK8841